T0130003

STUCK

IN A

SCHMUCK
A TRUE STORY

SOLEDAD CARRILLO

authorHOUSE®

AuthorHouse™
1663 Liberty Drive
Bloomington, IN 47403
www.authorhouse.com
Phone: 1 (800) 839-8640

Published by AuthorHouse   04/19/2018

ISBN: 978-1-5462-3910-9 (sc)
ISBN: 978-1-5462-3909-3 (e)

Library of Congress Control Number: 2018904876

Print information available on the last page.

This book is printed on acid-free paper.

INTRODUCTION

Stuck in a schmuck—that's a phrase I'll always remember. What does it mean? Hmmm. When I first heard it, it meant no hope, give up, or sorry, you're out of luck. It made me feel helpless, useless, tired, crazy, angry, and frustrated.

Did the person who directed that phrase at me simply mean, "Sorry, I can't help you"? It would have been much more professional of her if she had said that considering she was supposed to advocate for children in the special education department. But she chose to tell me, "I'm sorry, but you're just stuck in a schmuck."

Keep in mind that I had been anxiously waiting to hear from her for the previous ten days and I was anticipating good news. After that long wait and finally getting a call from her after having left several urgent messages on her voicemail, I was told I was simply stuck in a schmuck.

I had never heard that phrase before. What did her words mean? Since several months have passed, I have realized that this person was really telling me, "Go away. Don't bother me. I don't care about you or your child." At least that is what it felt like the day I got the call.

I was going to dedicate this book to her, who shall remain anonymous. She knows who she is. However, I dedicate this book to my three children—Ana, my oldest, Eddie, my middle child, and Belle, my youngest. They inspired me to share our story.

Because of them, I have discovered another side of me. I am not just a mother; I am also an advocate. I had to learn to assert my rights as a parent of a child with a learning disability. I had to learn that it was okay to disagree with a teacher, a principal, or a student counselor. I come from a culture that views teachers with such respect that it can be considered disrespectful to disagree with them, but I say to all the parents out there whose children have learning disabilities that it's okay to agree to disagree.

I want to believe that when children have learning disabilities, the majority of the educational team will search for the best plan to help them learn successfully. I experienced such a team with Eddie, but I experienced quite the opposite with Belle. I share our story to help families who are feeling lost, unheard, and frustrated understand that they have a say-so in their children's educational plan. I also hope our story will catch the attention of teachers so they will listen to the needs of special-needs children and their families.

Belle was briefly a middle school dropout because of the lack of support we received from her school. I hope our story is one of the few and that the percentage of indifferent teachers in special education departments are but a handful and that their indifference will not make a difference any longer.

CHAPTER 1

Another IEP

It's February 24, 2010. I'm meeting for the first time with my child's teachers regarding her progress and her IEP, her individual educational plan. I want to look my best today; I'm representing my girl, and I take that role very seriously, so appearance is important to me.

I'm wearing black slacks, a spark of royal blue as my top, and a matching black blazer and heels. My makeup is enough to notice but not too dark—just enough so I will look professional and be taken seriously. This means doing a little more walking on heels, something my feet are no longer accustomed to.

But I need to make the best impression. I have not really sat down with any of the teachers enough for them to know me; they know me only on paper. I'm sure that the impression they have of me based on my writing is not very pleasant and that they have defined me as a dominating parent who causes trouble when things do not go her way though my personality is on the meek side and I am rather friendly.

This is our first year in this school, one of the largest my daughter has attended. It is also the type of school I have always avoided. I never wanted my children to go to such a large middle school. There are so many kids; how can anyone keep track of them all? My children attended a small public school with only sixty kids per grade. Now, here's my youngest child attending a school where there are about five hundred eighth graders and five hundred seventh graders.

I do not know what to expect at today's meeting, but it has to be good. My Belle has managed to keep a grade point average at or above 3.0. We attended her honor-roll ceremony earlier this month. She had never been on any sort of honor list of any kind at school. I was the only parent with balloons! I kept them in the car to not embarrass her for being the only one with an over-the-top, ecstatic mom.

I took half the day off from work today to get home and freshen up. I made sure my makeup was just right. I gathered my notebook, got in my car, and arrived about half an hour early for the meeting.

When I arrive, I am greeted by Sandy the sucketary … I mean secretary. I walk in with confidence in spite of my insecurities and the tension I feel every time I walk into this office. Sandy lets them know I am here. I thank her and take a seat. I try not to hold grudges. I am sure Sandy is only doing what she is told. The first time I walked in there about eleven months ago to enroll my Belle, she was the first person I encountered, the first person to make me jump through hoops to get Belle enrolled. She had forced smiles when I continued to come back to the office to enroll Belle. She had stopped answering my calls. Maybe it was coincidental that after calling approximately three times and getting her voicemail each time, I decided to call minutes later using my friend's phone and Sandy graciously answered. She was most likely doing what she had been told, and we made it in the school in spite of that.

Ms. Lopez, my daughter's IEP teacher, greets us. She is a special education teacher and works closely with the students who have IEPs to ensure they are being properly supported in each class. She is very friendly and welcoming, and I am pleasantly surprised. She starts off by asking me where my daughter is.

I recall the last IEP meeting we had. My daughter had broken out in tears feeling humiliated and worthless. I explain to the teacher that I had asked her not to come because I would rather not have her hear anything negative since she is doing better and seems happier right now.

Ms. Lopez looks confused and asks, "What? She's a rock star! There is absolutely nothing negative to say about her. I wish she were here to listen to all the amazing feedback we have!"

I am surprised, but this is exactly the tone of the meeting for the next two hours. Ms. Lopez brings up her struggles but also her potential. I speak, she listens, and vice versa. We even laugh a few times. Belle's teachers arrive and give their concerns but also share Belle's strengths. It feels good not to be the only one able to see my daughter's strengths.

At the end, Ms. Lopez expresses that she is pleasantly surprised. She admits that after being assigned my daughter and viewing her file, she was somewhat apprehensive about meeting me. She tells me she is glad to have the opportunity to work with my daughter and me.

It turns out she knows my husband, who is a custodian at the school district she used to work for. Due to his exceptional work, he is recognized and appreciated by his coworkers. Ms. Lopez recognized my husband at the Back to School Night earlier in the year. She was surprised when she saw him and found out Belle was his daughter.

I ask myself if this makes a difference. Maybe it does. I'll never know. But the support and interest she gives my daughter feels authentic, and it has been a long time since I have felt like this about any of my daughter's teachers. Her support feels comforting, and I want to believe it's genuine.

After the meeting, Ms. Lopez notices my shoes and says, "Wow. I can't wear shoes that high anymore!" I notice she is wearing tennis shoes with a dress. I could have saved myself quite a bit of worrying if I had known the atmosphere would be so relaxed and welcoming.

We have quite a bit to celebrate. My husband and I take Belle out to her favorite restaurant to express our pride in her.

CHAPTER 2

No Child Is the Same, but Every Child Can Succeed

I consider being the mother of three children not a chore but a gift that has brought out the best in me. It has driven me to educate myself in spite of my lack of a college education. I struggled in school, but I completed high school and obtained a diploma through an independent study program. I went to school only once a week to submit my work for my high school remedial classes. I do not know what it feels like to walk across a stage and wear a cap and gown.

Every parent can testify that every child is different. Ana, my oldest, sailed through school and obtained a bachelor's degree in less than four years from the University of California. She had captured her teachers' attention from kindergarten on and was constantly praised for just being herself, a student who was academically inclined.

She had breezed through high school, and when she walked across the stage in her cap and gown, I felt I was walking across that stage right beside her. Attending her graduation from college three and a half years later was another proud moment. I may not have been the one with that cap and gown, but I finally felt the pride and joy of wearing them and getting ready to receive status as a college graduate.

Eddie was identified as having some learning issues in third grade. I was confused, worried, and frustrated when the school recommended holding him back. I thought, *Where did I go wrong? Is it my fault? Is it my husband's fault?* I thought I was raising my children the same, so I wondered why Ana was succeeding but Eddie wasn't. I had so many questions, but I was fortunate to have such a supportive staff of teachers and administrators.

My children were attending a small school, kindergarten through sixth grade, with only sixty students per grade. The support for my son started immediately. He was tested and discovered to have a learning disability in auditory processing. I was assured that he would be successful. That was all new to me, so I had many doubts and fears.

My son was assigned a special education teacher, Ms. Carroll, who had not only the degree to help struggling students but also a heart full of passion for them. She supported my son the moment he was approved for his individual IEP that would target his specific needs. That required exploring his learning style and what made it easier for him to succeed academically. With Ms. Carroll's support, Eddie was successful in the rest of his primary years in school and participated in almost all the honor-roll celebrations in his three years of middle school. He experienced some bumps in the road in high school, but he was still offered a place at a four-year university right after he graduated. Eddie won't obtain his degree in three and one half years—most likely in five—but if that works for him, it works for me.

Belle, my youngest, struggled socially as well as academically. When she was in kindergarten, her teacher was very concerned that she was showing signs of Asperger's syndrome as well as battling a learning disability. I was baffled and caught off guard. Her teacher told me that Belle didn't make much eye contact and that she tended to talk about the same subjects—dogs and cats. She loved to draw them and talk about them. I of course immediately took her to be evaluated. However, the only issue we found was that she also struggled with auditory processing and would qualify for IEP support in school.

CHAPTER 3

The Powerful Seed

I thank my Eddie for all his hard work. He does not realize it, but his hard work planted a seed in me that was nourished during all the obstacles he confronted in middle school and high school by his determination, hope, energy, and enthusiasm.

So when I heard that phrase "stuck in a schmuck," I was ready for it. Those words had no room in me due to the powerful seed my son had helped nourish in me. I was nervous when he started middle school; his obliviousness to the fact that he had to turn homework in on time kept me on edge. He made it into high school though it wasn't easy. I tried everything to keep his focus. He was on the volleyball team and folkloric dance team. I hoped that if he got involved in such activities, he would enjoy school. I even kept him in the same school when we moved about fifteen miles away. Driving him there made me about ten minutes late for work every day because of his lack of enthusiasm in the morning, but we did it.

I'll never forget the look on his face when he was

accepted to a four-year state university. That made me remember the day when he was a sophomore in high school and we had to drive Ana back to her university. She gave her brother a tour of the campus, and he said, "Like if I would ever make it to a place like this." Remembering those words now is just as painful as was listening to them for the first time.

I said, "Don't ever underestimate yourself! You're just as capable, but you have to believe it!" I was worried, but I couldn't let him know that. So there we were reading his acceptance letter to this four-year state university six hours away from home!

But he had to finish high school, and that wasn't easy for him or me. My blood pressure went up and down with his grades, and being late for work just added to my stress.

On his last day of high school, I was on a cloud. I compared myself to Snow White, who awoke to the chirping of birds knowing an evil queen was out there wanting to end her life, but she managed to whistle and sing her way through her day.

I was overjoyed to think that after I dropped him off that day, I'd never be late for work again for that reason. Nothing was going to ruin that day for me. We got there, and I hurried him along to class. As he was walking, I remembered him as a five-year-old walking to kindergarten and waving goodbye proudly wearing his Batman backpack. I cried all the way to work. I realize now that my boy's struggles actually had much to do with my strength and hope.

So Belle's learning disability, which was similar to

Eddie's, worried me but didn't scare me. I no longer had questions about who was at fault or where we could have gone wrong. Instead, my question was, "So when can we get started on the right educational plan to start building the bridge to college for Belle?"

CHAPTER 4

Rude Awakening

Kindergarten through third grade were not too difficult for Belle. We knew she was struggling, but we were pinpointing where she was struggling the most. She had friends and seemed to enjoy school. She actually taught herself to read before first grade. In the summer after kindergarten, she mastered reading English and Spanish. However, due to her auditory processing and her struggle to retain information, her reading comprehension suffered. Fortunately, we had Ms. Carroll, who was working closely with her. She kept her focused and positive through those years.

But when Belle was in the fifth grade, she became rather quiet in school. When I would pick her up from school, I'd see her playing with younger children. I'd ask her where her classmates were, and she would say they were playing something she didn't care for.

Ours was such a close-knit community; everyone knew each other, so hanging out with friends other than classmates was not necessarily unusual. I wasn't too worried about that. I focused more on making sure she was academically ready for sixth grade, her last year in elementary school. She was not held back as my son had been though she had similar learning difficulties.

I was excited when Belle began sixth grade; her teacher was one of the best. I felt fortunate to have such a dedicated teacher on my daughter's side. On her first day of school, I introduced myself to her teacher. I wanted to make sure she was aware of my daughter's learning obstacles. I wanted to set up a meeting so we could get started on building a bridge to college for her.

We met about a month after school started. It was apparent that my daughter was well below her grade level; she struggled mainly in math. But Ms. Carroll, her IEP teacher, was optimistic that Belle could reach the goals she had set for her. Ms. Carroll's enthusiasm nourished that seed in me.

Unfortunately, her teacher, the one I had felt so fortunate to have, was not impressed with any of my daughter's progress. She simply focused on what she was not able to do. She showed no concern for or interest in working on any plans to help my daughter prepare for middle school. She sat stone-faced during this meeting and gave little input and showed no interest in being part of our team. She seemed frustrated; her only suggestion was that Belle be held back.

That was my rude awakening; Belle had been assigned supposedly one of the best teachers, whom everyone loved, but this teacher had no faith in Belle. In addition, Belle did not have any friends in the sixth grade, and no one noticed that but me.

One day after school, she looked sad. Once she was in the car, she burst into tears. My daughter was alone in this close-knit community school. The only person who seemed to believe in her besides her family was Ms. Carroll, her IEP teacher.

At one of our last conferences, her teacher mentioned that math was not the only area in which my daughter was struggling. She said she believed Belle did not understand simple directions. I asked for an example. She told me that the children had had hot chocolate in class one day and had been asked to put their mugs in the sink after they had finished their hot chocolate. She told me that Belle had not done that; she had put her mug under her desk. I was surprised to hear that, but I knew there had to be a reasonable explanation.

I brought up the incident with Belle that evening. She told me that her father had given her a cup to take to school that day, not a mug. She was embarrassed that she was the only one with a cup rather than a mug and hadn't wanted the other kids to know that. My poor Belle had a very good reason for not following her teacher's instructions. I'm not saying she was right to do that, but it certainly wasn't because she hadn't understood her teacher.

The first opportunity I had, I explained Belle's reasoning to the teacher and pointed out that it hadn't been a matter of Belle not knowing how to follow directions. I told her that if she had only tried to find out what the problem was, she would not have jumped to such a drastic conclusion. She looked at me with the same stone face she always looked at me with and did not respond.

But everyone loved this teacher. She was supposedly one of the best. I started recalling all the great teachers my academically independent Ana had had. All her teachers had been wonderful. They praised her and always took time to tell me what a great student she was. I'd received nothing but positive feedback from her teachers. My academically inclined Ana brought out the passion in all of them.

I'd never witnessed a teacher expressing indifference toward a student until my Belle's sixth-grade teacher did that. I realized she had no concern for my struggling student, only those students who made her job easy. My child required one-on-one attention. Sometimes, Belle needed to have lessons repeated not just twice but maybe three or four times for her to understand, but did that make her a horrible student? She went to school every day on time. She was the best-behaved student in the class, but because she struggled to learn, she was not a great student.

The goal is to get every child to learn. Our state's policy was that no child would be left behind, but my child was being left behind. Nobody seemed to notice that except for me. Belle brought out the true colors of this supposedly great teacher, and unfortunately, she brought out the true colors of many more teachers to come.

CHAPTER 5

Middle School

By the end of Belle's sixth grade, I was desperate, alone, and anxious. Ms. Carroll was the only one at school who motivated Belle and me to understand that just because Belle had a learning disability didn't mean she couldn't learn, but Ms. Carroll was retiring at the end of that year.

I had to choose between keeping Belle in that district or moving her to another district even if it meant driving a little farther. It would at least be a fresh start. My husband and I were very active parents there for the fifteen years. Ana and Eddie had gone there for kindergarten through sixth grade; it had been their home away from home, but for Belle, it was her hell away from home.

When I picked up Ana and Eddie from school, I was constantly greeted by parents, teachers, and students. My children were well known, and so was I. But I started to feel like an outsider there. I could not imagine feeling like that all day. It could have been my imagination, but even the parents of Belle's classmates barely acknowledged me.

Knowing that Belle was feeling the same exclusion was very painful.

Some of the girls in Belle's class were maturing, and some were even wearing makeup. My Belle was not interested in makeup, magazines, or clothing styles. She still enjoyed sparkles on her shoes and clothes. Even Allie, her best friend, had moved on. She and Belle had called each other best friends in kindergarten and first grade, and it just stayed with my daughter that Allie was her best friend. But when I'd pick Belle up, she was never playing with Allie. When I asked about Allie, Belle would say that Allie was playing a game she didn't care to play.

Years before that, Belle was occasionally invited to Allie's house and even to a couple of sleepovers. I would usually take her there but then pick her up before they went to sleep because Belle was not ready to spend the night elsewhere.

In the fourth grade, she did find the courage to finally spend the night. I felt great that she was enjoying being a 'tween. But after the sleepover, I noticed she had some sticky white stuff in her hair. I asked her about it, and she broke down. She had woken up the night at the sleepover with white goo all over her hair. The girls had done that to her while she was sleeping. So yes, Allie had moved on.

I went over the pros and cons with Belle of switching schools. One of the pros was that we would no longer have to lie about our address. You see, we had moved fifteen miles away and were in a different school district. My poor Belle had to memorize the wrong address in kindergarten. I know it was not very honest of me to do that, but my older children were still in school when we moved and I didn't want them to change school districts. Eddie was doing so well, and I didn't want to interrupt his success. Therefore, being able to use our actual address was a good thing about changing schools. I told her no one would know her and it would be easier for her to make new friends. She knew she did not have any friends in her class then, and even her teacher was completely disconnected from her.

So I took the advice of someone I trusted and took my child charter-school shopping.

CHAPTER 6

From Public to Charter

I'd heard of charter schools, but I wasn't sure exactly how they worked. Our kindergarten-through-sixth-grade school was all we knew. Belle and I attended an orientation together, and I felt so much positive energy in the room. They talked about preparing all the students not just for high school but also for college. They promised a great individual plan for every student. They emphasized that because every child was different, every child needed an individualized learning plan. I thought Belle's bridge to college was under construction. This new school was sixth to ninth grade. Though Belle had completed sixth grade, they welcomed her as a sixth grader.

During the orientation, I saw excitement in Belle's eyes. It had been a long time since I had seen her face light up like that. She said, "I want to go to this school." That was enough for me to make the change from public to charter.

We were excited to have a fresh start at a place where no one would see my child branded with any negativity.

In fact, this was a new school, so all the students were new. No more hiding where we lived and picking up our school mail at someone else's house once a month. It felt so right.

At the beginning of the school year, I set up an IEP meeting with her teachers and her new IEP teacher. It was the first month of school. All the teachers including the principal were so positive and welcoming. There was no negativity during that meeting. Our plan was to see where Belle was struggling and build her up from there. My seed was getting nourishment again.

But as the semester progressed, Belle's test scores did not. She rarely asked for help with homework. I noticed that her math and writing assignments were equivalent to what she had done in second grade. Her IEP teacher assured me that it was a strategy they used to figure out where exactly she had fallen behind. They told me that as soon as they were able to figure out where she had fallen through the cracks, they would work from there and bring her up to grade level. Though it made sense, it didn't feel right.

But my daughter was making friends there and adapting socially, so that made it easier. And I ran into a familiar face at that school. A young assistant teacher who had been one of my Ana's classmates was working there. I asked her in confidence her opinion about the school. She hesitated, but she was honest. She told me the sooner I took Belle out of there the better. Because it was new, the school focused on making sure students scored very high on the state standard tests because their funding depended on that.

My Belle had always scored below average and at times far below average. I was curious about how they would prepare her to score well considering her needs. The school was too new and not equipped to teach a child with learning difficulties. I felt so guilty and lost. How could I move my child? She had problems making friends and was below grade level. By the second semester, I started charter-school shopping again.

In the spring, I took Belle to an orientation at a charter school that was seventh through eighth grade. It was not even in the same city I lived in, but I thought it would be ideal if she could attend that school because it seemed ready to offer her support and help. Belle would start off as a seventh grader with all the other new seventh graders.

The orientation was powerful. They talked about the 100 percent high school graduation rate of their students and said that all their students were prepared for college and that many went to the most prestigious universities in the country. I wanted to make sure this school was the right one for us, so after the director of the school finished her presentation, I raised my hand and asked, "Can students with IEPs attend here?" Without hesitation she responded, "Of course. All students are able to attend here." I realize now that she had to say that to a room full of parents. But at the time, Belle and I felt this school was the one. We decided to apply and enter the lottery though I wasn't hopeful. But my daughter wanted this so badly, and I wanted it for her. I told her that it would happen if it was meant to happen.

Two months later, I received the call. We got in!

CHAPTER 7

From Charter to Charter

That was one of the best calls we had received in a long time. We had heard how difficult it was to get into that school, but there we were at orientation for the new seventh graders and their families. I felt sure that this school would support Belle.

We had a presentation about the student schedule, received the school calendar, and covered all the facets of a typical seventh-grade agenda. One by one, the students were tested for their proficiency in math and English. My Belle was one of the last to be called, and I was left waiting. After the testing, I would meet briefly with the principal.

As I was waiting, one teacher approached me. We made small talk, and then he asked about Belle. He said, "Your daughter must really be on top of things if she's going to be coming here!"

I thought that was odd, but I said, "Yes, she's on top of things in spite of her learning difficulties. She has an IEP." As soon as I said that, I realized he had already known that. He asked why she was not in a regular public school where she could get more support.

I couldn't believe what I was hearing. He said charter schools were not funded enough to support IEP students. I was speechless! His approach felt suspicious. I felt he was trying to discourage me from enrolling Belle there. But he just made me angry, and I said, "Since this school guarantees success for a hundred percent of its students, I feel we're in the right place!"

When the principal called me in, the first thing I mentioned was what that teacher had said to me. That was the first of many endless complaints.

When the school year started, I was elated that Belle was attending one of the best charter schools in the county. Belle had even made a friend who was anxiously waiting for her when I dropped her off. I was once again excited that Belle would have experienced and caring teachers who would be working with her.

I met with Belle's IEP teacher and a few of her teachers at the beginning of the year. I had expected to meet them all, but most of them had opted out at the last minute. This school was much more rigorous and demanding than Belle was used to. The curriculum forced her to work longer and harder. She gained some stamina from this, which I still think is wonderful, and her IEP teacher was a breath of fresh air. She invested quality time with my Belle working one on one. She initiated almost monthly meetings with me, and our meetings were always positive. She brought up Belle's struggles but also her good qualities. I learned that Belle was handling math on a third-grade level. I had actually just received the state testing results my daughter had taken at the first charter school; she had scored average or above average on them in every subject including math. I was skeptical about that since she had always scored basic or below. I asked her how Belle could have scored so high on the state test.

The IEP teacher did not say exactly but insinuated that they could have "accidentally" given her an easier test or left the answers within her sight. I recalled a conversation I had had with the young assistant at the first charter school. It was disappointing to think there was so much corruption that nobody knew about.

Later on that year, the charter school we had left became front-page news; it was being recognized for having one of the highest testing results for our state school tests. There was no way to prove my daughter's test scores were false, so I simply moved on.

This IEP teacher on the other hand helped my daughter in the seventh grade. That year was a blessing because of this IEP teacher. I cannot say much for the rest of her teachers since the majority had to be reminded that my Belle had an IEP. They rarely showed up at any of the IEP meetings we held that year.

My Belle was not enjoying all the extra time she had to invest in her homework, but she did learn what was expected of her to succeed in school. She was able to maintain a C average with the assistance of this amazing IEP teacher for seventh grade. But just before Belle started eighth grade, her IEP teacher told me that she has been promoted and that Belle would have someone new in eighth grade.

CHAPTER 8

Eighth Grade Part I

Right at the beginning of Belle's eighth-grade year, I noticed she wasn't receiving much attention. A month passed, and the school had not yet hired a new IEP teacher to work with her. A substitute was available but did not invest nearly half the time with my Belle as her IEP teacher had the previous year. In fact, they let Belle decide when she wanted to check in with the IEP teacher. I started to notice immediately a decline in Belle's effort and level of motivation.

I wasn't informed when an IEP teacher was hired. He had been there more than a month before I found out, and that was because Belle mentioned it to me. I called the school and left a message for the new IEP teacher. My first conversation on the phone with him was disheartening. He talked about how Belle has not been paying attention and was always talking about what she enjoyed doing in her free time. He said he thought what she talked about and did in class was kind of weird. I was stunned. I did not know how to react. But in spite of my anger, I decided to meet with him and give him the benefit of the doubt. I would then decide whether to start complaining.

We had our first meeting shortly after. I was not impressed with the way he presented his input about my child. He seemed so tired and looked as if he didn't want to be there. He didn't have any plan for helping Belle raise her current Ds and Fs. The principal was present; he was slouched and periodically glanced at his phone as if hoping for a distraction. I was convinced Belle and I were alone again. No one seemed to care that my Belle had Ds and Fs and no friends. We had a couple of meetings thereafter, and Belle was asked to attend them.

Each time, she had to endure listening to how poorly she was doing and that she was not doing enough. The IEP teacher and the principal along with some of the teachers who would occasionally attend would focus on what she was not doing. They would tell her that because she was not asking for help, they could not help her. That was their way of saying Belle was failing due to her lack of effort and was therefore the one at fault. Each time, Belle would break down in tears after we left those meetings. The last time she broke down, I vowed never to make her attend another IEP meeting.

The same trend started—she was no longer hanging out with anyone when I would pick her up. She started looking depressed and would complain about having to go to school. By the time the second semester started, it was obvious that Belle would not be ready for high school. I found it useless at that point to meet with the principal or the IEP teacher. Her IEP was being ignored in all her classes. She did not understand half of the material, and none of the teachers was checking with her to make sure she did. That was specifically written on her IEP. My child was being extremely neglected. I felt like a nuisance when I would suggest a different IEP plan. I actually received an email from her IEP teacher suggesting that it was likely she would be better off at a regular public high school and register for remedial classes; that was the extent of his plan.

Our bridge started to crumble. I felt guilty and angry at myself for having moved my child to a charter school. My mind would race—*How can I help my Belle?* She was depressed and did not want to be there. I could not just move her in the middle of the second semester. So my husband, my child, and I started team building ourselves.

We knew she would not be ready for high school academically or emotionally. I researched public middle schools in our area and learned they were much larger than the schools we were used to. She had always belonged to a class of fewer than sixty students per grade. These middle schools had about five hundred students in seventh and eighth grades.

I talked to Belle about repeating eighth grade at a public school closer to home. At first, she was shocked at my suggestion, but my husband and I assured her we would let her give us her input in the decision. We let her talk to a therapist and to her close family members, and we made a list of the pros and cons. After two months of contemplating the matter, Belle felt that the best plan for her would be to repeat eighth grade at a neighborhood school.

CHAPTER 9

Feeling Lost

In the beginning of March, Belle decided to put her high school career on hold; that's what we called it. We also called it an extra year of being a kid and another year to get ready for high school. Everyone who knew Belle agreed that was the best plan for our child, and Belle realized that as well.

So after we decided what we were going to do, I emailed the director and the principal of her school. I brought up her current failing grades. She had ended her first semester with Fs in all her core classes. I brought up how we just needed a letter recommending that she repeat eighth grade so I could register her as an eighth grader in our neighborhood public middle school. I felt hopeful and positive that this experienced director of education would agree that was a great plan to help my child succeed in high school. I presented my request not expecting the prompt negative response. The director simply said no; she would not let Belle repeat eighth grade.

Neither the director nor the principal offered to meet

me; they just immediately decided that they would not hold my child back. She would just have to move on to high school. The director stated that as far as she was concerned, my daughter was passing and would not be held back. I of course responded that she left me no choice but to appeal her decision. Her response was that there was no appeal process for that.

This email conversation left me numb, fearful, anxious, confused, angry—so many emotions. I spent the following weeks browsing the web to learn the rights my child and I were entitled to, and I called numerous attorneys. Most of them were sympathetic and listened, but all I heard was that it would be tough to convince the state to hold back an eighth grader. In addition, it would be expensive.

I spoke to advocates and spent countless hours reading on my own. I was searching for someone who could help me, but the more I read, the more of a blur it was to me. I was overwhelmed by all the information I had found; it seemed too complicated for me.

I have not mentioned my husband too often for a reason. His first language is Spanish, and all the information I found was in English. He gave me moral support, but he could not help me comprehend what I was reading. I told him that we would have no choice but to take a second mortgage on our home and hire an attorney. By May, I was convinced I would find an attorney and my Belle would not go to high school that fall.

I wanted to prove that this charter school was not following my daughter's IEP. I even contacted other families with students who had IEPs at this charter school and asked them about their experience with the charter school. I could not believe what they shared. They too had been approached by a teacher at orientation and had been told that public schools would be better for their children. I brought this up to the attorneys I spoke to, but they said I would have to gather many families to open any kind of a case accusing them of discreetly discouraging families with IEP students.

I decided to reach out to someone from my children's past—Ms. Carroll. Though she was retired, she agreed to accompany me to my last IEP meeting with the charter school. There was a lot of tension in the room. They did not seem very happy that I had brought an advocate, but they did not have a choice in the matter. The director was there along with someone I had never seen. He held a very high position in the schools in the area and worked with this charter school as well. I felt much more confident in that room with Ms. Carroll by my side; I trusted her because she had the knowledge to navigate this process, and that made me feel less intimidated. However, nothing was resolved at that meeting. The director and principal were adamant about not holding my daughter back. After the meeting, Ms. Carroll advised me to simply register my daughter at the neighborhood middle school without the retention letter.

That's what I did. Since we had changed schools quite a bit the last couple of years, I already knew what the school would need from me. I made sure that Belle's immunization card was updated and that I had her birth certificate. I brought three verifications that I lived in the district. I was ready, or so I thought. I took a deep breath and walked in the office.

The secretary greeted me kindly, and I said I wanted to enroll my daughter there as an eighth grader. She of course asked where she was currently attending. I explained the situation to her about how she was failing eighth grade and therefore needed to repeat the grade at that school, which was our neighborhood school.

She immediately changed her expression and became cautious as she spoke. It got a little tense. She told me that enrolling Belle there was not likely to happen unless I received a letter of retention from the charter school. I left the office feeling helpless and ready to take out a loan to go attorney shopping. All I could think about was that my child was not going to high school the next year, and if our neighborhood school would not accept her, Belle would be a middle school drop out!

CHAPTER 10

Middle School Dropout

At the end of May, finals were approaching. I asked the director again for a letter of retention but to no avail. I decided not to send my child to her final exams the last week of school.

The end of the school year came and went. Belle was a middle school dropout. I was barely mentally surviving. I went to work, cooked, and cleaned, but it was so robotic. I decided to contact the superintendent of my middle school district. I was transferred to someone who played a big role in advocating for children in the special education department, and I explained my situation. She seemed to listen; her concerned tone of voice gave me hope. She guaranteed that she would discuss my daughter's file and get back to me in a couple of weeks. I had no choice but to wait. In the meantime, I browsed the Internet for any special-education attorneys who might help me.

Every June, my family and I participated in a spiritual family retreat. I was in no mood to go that year and was already making excuses for not attending. Belle really wanted to go, which is the only reason I went. I had still not heard from the director of the special ed department. I was constantly checking my phone to make sure it was on and not on silent. I had left several messages. Although I was anxious, I was hopeful that after reviewing my daughter's transcript, she would agree that it was in her best interests to repeat eighth grade.

It so happened that on Friday evening on our way to our spiritual retreat, my phone rang. It was the district! I was so happy to hear from her. I was already thanking God in my head for letting me start out that weekend with some good news. However, that's when I heard that most bizarre and meaningless phrase for the first time— she said, "I'm sorry, but you're just stuck in a schmuck."

I didn't know how to respond. I was in shock. I asked her to explain herself. She stated that Belle would have to move on to high school because the charter school would not retain her. Her condescending words were not convincing. I didn't feel she was really trying to help me. I sensed almost a relief in her voice. I asked her what she needed for my daughter to be accepted as an eighth grader, and she mentioned that letter of retention. I asked her to give me that in writing, which she agreed to do.

CHAPTER 11

I Found an Attorney

My spiritual retreat started out pretty rocky. I was on an emotional roller-coaster. I was ready to turn around to go back home, but something inside me told me to stay.

I of course was not in the mood to be around anybody. I did not volunteer to speak at the retreat that year; I decided I would be just a listener. I had no idea who the speakers were going to be. Normally, I attended preparation meetings and was involved in planning the programs, but I had not done so that year because I was so overwhelmed by my daughter's situation.

By Saturday, the second day of the retreat, we were getting ready to listen to the next speaker. When they announced who this speaker was, I looked up and saw a young girl I had known since she had been a toddler. Reya was about four years older than Belle. She reminded me of Belle in many ways. She would rarely speak up, giver her opinion, or participate very much; she seemed to not want to be noticed. My tears started coming down. There was nothing too emotional about what she said;

she talked about the importance of communication. Her presentation was anything but perfect—she nervously laughed too much, and some of what she said didn't make sense. I don't know why I was crying so much. As she continued her presentation, I realized I was meant to be at this retreat; I was meant to see and hear Reya give her presentation.

Some would say I was listening to a little voice within, and that's fine with me. But my little voice that told me to stay was God. I felt He was asking me, "If I was able to get this far with Reya, do you not trust Me enough to help you confront these school districts? Trust Me to be your attorney. I won't charge you a dime."

I suddenly felt much better; I was able to enjoy the rest of the retreat. But all I could think about was getting back home so I could look up my parental rights and do what it took to assure that Belle got whatever help she needed.

CHAPTER 12

Fighting Goliath

I started browsing the web for all my rights and how to exercise them on the evening we got back from the retreat. I reread all the material I had read before, and it started making sense. I no longer felt I needed an attorney to help me comprehend the process. I downloaded all the forms and filled out the paperwork. I printed all the emails including the response from the director of the charter school that read, "There is no appeal process." Thank goodness they had left a paper trail because I printed out a number of emails showing their noncompliance with my daughter's IEP. I got my packet together and mailed it to the special education office, which looks out for the rights of children with special education needs.

About a week later, I received the letter from the "stuck in a schmuck" advocate woman which read, "In order for your child to be accepted in our school district, we will need something in writing clearly stating that she is being retained from her current school." At that moment, I felt it would have been impossible to obtain, but I no longer felt helpless. I tried not to think that Belle was currently not enrolled anywhere at the moment. I had tried contacting the person who had attended my daughter's IEP meeting to which Ms. Carroll accompanied us. That person held an important positon for the district that worked with the charter school. He called me back.

It so happened that he was also a friend of the director to the charter school. I told him I filed a complaint with one of the head offices in the department of education. He told me he would try talking to his colleague.

That week, I received an email from him stating that my daughter would be held back, and I was so excited. I called up Sandy, the secretary, and told her I had a letter of retention I would bring to her. She looked annoyed when I came in but took the letter and said she would forward it to the advocate in the special ed department I was working with—the "stuck in a schmuck" woman.

A week later, I called Sandy, and she said the letter was not sufficient; her transcript also needed to say she had been retained. I called up the friend of the director from the charter school, and he said he had thought the email would have been enough. He said he would contact the director of the charter school to see if she would officially retain her on her transcript.

He called back to say that the director was not willing to do that. He said he was trying to convince his colleague to retain my daughter. I said that that left me no choice but to continue with the formal complaint.

Within a month, I got a response to my complaint; they had opened an investigation and set a mediation date with the charter school. Finally, someone else seemed to be caring! It was nerve-racking, but I felt so much better. I was confident I would be able to gather information that would prove how the school had been breaking the law by not complying with my child's IEP. I couldn't sleep the night before the mediation because I was nervous. It was the end of July, the start of the school year was about two weeks away, and my daughter was not enrolled anywhere.

We got to the mediation twenty minutes early, met the mediator outside, and walked in together. The director escorted us to an office. She looked very serious. The principal was there as well, but he barely turned to say hello to us. The atmosphere was tense, negative. I cannot disclose what we discussed; we signed an agreement that what was said there would remain confidential. The hostile environment was uncomfortable, but my husband and I remained calm.

The mediation lasted about forty minutes. The outcome was the best news we could ever have had. Ironically, the best news was receiving a sealed envelope with her transcripts showing Belle had been retained and could not move on to high school. All I could think about was getting the sealed envelope to Sandy the secretary.

We drove directly to the school I wanted to enroll her in. I was beyond happy. Finally, my Belle will be enrolled in school again. We walked into the office, and I handed Sandy the sealed envelope. I told her it contained my daughter's transcript showing retention. She looked shocked, but I felt confident. She stated she would have the advocate who was working with me get back to me to see what she had decided. I thought that was odd; what was there to decide? I thanked her anyway and left.

A week passed, and I still had heard nothing. It was four days until the beginning of the school year, and Sandy was not answering my calls; all I got was her voicemail. Something suddenly didn't feel right. I felt uneasy. My husband told me it was my imagination. I decided to reread the letter from the "stuck in a schmuck" advocate that said what she needed for my daughter to be enrolled at our middle school. I suddenly noticed the last sentence—"The final decision will be ours." I felt that after defeating one Goliath, I had to go up against another.

The next day, I called Sandy but got just her voicemail. I borrowed a friend's phone and called again; Sandy graciously answered and sounded surprised to hear my voice. She said she had not heard back from the advocate I had been working with.

An inner voice told me to search the web again. It was not a charter school, so I figured there had to be a local office that could help me. I made a couple of calls and found the office that represented children from our neighborhood school. I explained our situation to someone who listened and seemed very concerned. He assured me that someone from the school would call me that day.

Within an hour, Sandy called me to "congratulate" me—my daughter has been accepted. All my closest friends and family got a text from me stating, "I am not stuck in a schmuck!" They all knew what I meant.

At the end of the day, I got a call from the friend of the charter school director; he asked if I had gotten my daughter enrolled, and I said, "Yes I did!" He seemed surprised and confided in me that it was a good thing I had had called and spoken to the person at that office. He told me that they had had no intention of accepting my daughter. That confirmed my suspicions. The uneasiness I felt had not been my imagination. I was thankful for the voice inside me.

It is disappointing how deceiving these people in charge could be. They pretended to listen to me and told me they were concerned. They told me how nothing could be done and how their "hands were tied." I was thrilled nevertheless, and nobody could take that away!

CHAPTER 13

Eighth Grade Part II

It was scary starting eighth grade all over again; I was scared Belle would be ignored in the midst of such a large group of kids. Within the first two weeks of school, I did my thing—I contacted her IEP teacher to make sure she knew who I was, and I emailed her teachers to make sure they were aware of her IEP.

My child started coming home happy, carefree, and confident, but I was not going to let my guard down. Her grades were pretty impressive—As and Bs—but I was not convinced. I received her first progress report by the end of the sixth week, and she seemed to be on top of every subject!

It was a joy to see her excited about school again. She joined the Latino club and tried out for cross-country. She didn't stay with cross-country, but I was proud that she had decided to try it. She participated in all her spirit days, and she was learning and having fun.

I started that school year with my radar on high alert and gloves on ready to tackle any issue or anyone who was not attending to Belle's needs or violating her rights by not complying with her IEP. By the end of the first semester, I started feeling more at ease with the positive and bubbly personality Belle was expressing. Going to school was no longer a forceful task. In fact, our biggest dilemma in the morning was how she was going to do her hair!

At the beginning of the second semester, I received a text from Belle while she was in school. It was a picture of an invitation letter to participate in the honor roll ceremony. I cannot even describe what I felt. I went home that day and gave my Belle the biggest high five, a hug, and a great number of kisses!

I asked her to describe to me the moment they handed this invitation to her. What she said was so endearing: "When they gave this to me, I didn't even know what it was since I had never seen one of these before. But when I saw that I'd made the honor roll, I thought I was gonna faint! Finally, someone cares about the work I do!"

Those were the words of a student who had attended a well-known and loved k-through-eighth-grade public school and a prestigious, established charter school. It amazed me that she had felt nobody ever cared about her work. We proudly attended honor roll night later that month!

CHAPTER 14

The Foundation Has Been Laid

We are toward the end of eighth grade now. A graduation gown has been purchased, a yearbook has been ordered, and a celebration party is being planned. We still have high school ahead of us, but the foundation for our bridge to it has been built and is a strong one.

I am happy and proud that Belle completed a second year of eighth grade with such dignity. I feel a huge sense of relief; I am exhausted emotionally, but I am so grateful. My Belle had almost been robbed of her middle school promotion experience. Because she had Ds and Fs, she would not have been allowed to participate in her promotion had she moved on to high school. She would not have experienced pride and a sense of accomplishment; she would have started high school feeling excluded.

I am so grateful to see my Belle proudly wearing her promotion gown. I reflect on those words *stuck in a schmuck*; they were telling me to give up. I am actually grateful for that director's choice of words—they empowered me with determination and stamina and helped me discover the advocate in me.

I am so proud of my children. Ana had had pretty smooth sailing through school; because of that, I had witnessed the passion she brought out in her teachers. Eddie had struggled and had to work harder than many students to graduate from high school, but he earned a spot in a four-year university! He showed me that you don't have to be a straight-A student to make it to college. There was a special seed planted in me because of his success that later helped me fight for Belle.

Belle, my rock star, proved that all her pessimistic and indifferent teachers were wrong. She demonstrates that no one education plan fits all or even most students. Every child is different, and every child can succeed with the proper support from special, passionate teachers. Teachers with good hearts as well as degrees can motivate struggling students and make achievement a reality.

I had told Belle when we applied to the second charter school, "If it's meant to be, it will happen." Although we experienced a horrible reality that occurs to students with special educational needs, I still feel it was meant to be. Belle was able to repeat eighth grade and participate with students who were slightly younger. Her emotional maturity is not quite at the level of that of the average child her age, so I knew that being with a younger group of students would benefit her.

I have developed and have learned so much about myself. I discovered how passionate an advocate I could be. I have a strong desire to communicate with and help other parents. I have become more vigilant and aware of what I sign at IEP meetings. My daughter found a "best friend" in her second year of eighth grade. We do not know what the future holds, but we are much better prepared to help Belle be successful in high school.

I do not mean to discourage families from having their children attend charter schools; those Belle had attended had excellent academic programs. I wanted to share our experience of how my daughter had almost been forced to move on to high school despite her not being ready for that. I wanted to share how I had not taken no for an answer.

I want other families to know there is a process they can go through when they do not agree with the decisions made for their children's education. I want to convey to parents that they have a say-so and that their voices can be heard and can make a difference.

When a child has a learning disability, his or her parents still hold a great part of the decision making rights and responsibilities for their child's education; they are still the ones who know what is best for their child. Professionals have the experience to guide them, and parents can positively collaborate with them. Even when the route to success is challenging, with the right support of parents and educators, that success is inevitable. We do not know what the future holds, but we are more aware and prepared to help my Belle succeed in high school.

I never knew what "stuck in a schmuck" meant, and if I really think about it, I still don't.

All You Need

When the doors are closing and no one seems to care
When your bridge is crumbling and you're running out of air
It's okay to be afraid but don't give up—stay strong
It's okay to cry a little but not for very long
But not for very long ...

(chorus)

All you need is to believe and listen to that voice
The one that's saying, "I believe in you"
All you need is to believe and recognize that voice
Keep listening and you'll believe it too

You may not be the one who shines everywhere you go
You may run into many who will make you feel alone
It doesn't matter what they think—you'll always be a star
It doesn't matter what they say—believe in who you are
Believe in who you are ...

(chorus)

All you need is to believe and listen to that voice
The one that's saying, "I believe in you"
All you need is to believe and recognize that voice
Keep listening and you'll believe it too

ABOUT THE AUTHOR

I am a mother of three. Two have completed college, and my son, who has a learning disability, made the Dean's list. My youngest, who also has a learning disability, is still in high school.

What do you do when your child is struggling in school? How do you handle when school officials tell you that your child cannot cope mainstream? How do you react when you learn your child has a learning disability? Do you still think about college for your child? Of course you do!

Mine is a true story about how children with learning disabilities can indeed succeed. Mine is a true story about how I navigated and even went against school administrators to obtain the best plan for my child.

Printed in the United States
By Bookmasters